ME, MYSELF & I

D0248656

MY PROFILE

DIG. QUESTION.
PONDER. WONDER. CHALLENGE.
Cross-examine. Grill. Interrogate.
Investigate. Needle. Query.

QUIZ YOURSELF TO CREATE YOUR OWN PROFILE.

WRITE HERE WRITE NOW

Nicole LaRue AND Naomi Davis Lee

chronicle books · san francisco

OBSERVE. BRAINSTORM.

QUESTION. IMAGINE. write.

ILLUSTRATE.

EXPLORE. COLLECT. DEVELOP.

DOCUMENT. PLAY. DESIGN.

DO ALL OF THESE THINGS, DEAR READER, AUTHOR, ARTIST, INVENTOR, RISK-TAKER, CREATOR, INK-SLINGER, WORDSMITH! DOCUMENT YOUR PAST. EXPLORE YOUR FUTURE. SKETCH YOUR FRIENDS. PROBE YOUR FAMILY. SCOUT YOUR COMMUNITY. DESIGN YOURSELF!

full name :

date :

hometown :

school :

birthday:

nickname:

blog:

NOTE:

☐ girl ☐ boy

☐ superhero

☐ other

circle one [or all]

What face do you have today?

SMOOCH

CHEEKY

SUSPICIOUS

DOWNER

SWEET THING

SLEEPY

SNOOZIN'

BIG GRIN

HE SAID/SHE SAID

PUT PEN TO PAPER

~ WRITE A LETTER ~

TO AN IMAGINARY OR REAL PERSON.

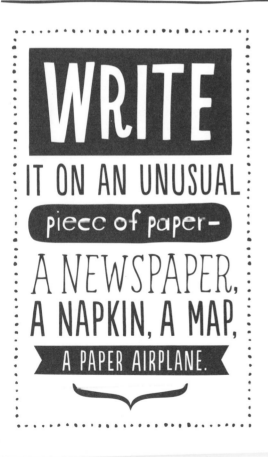

WRITE IT ON AN UNUSUAL *piece of paper*— A NEWSPAPER, A NAPKIN, A MAP, A PAPER AIRPLANE.

HERE'S AN **EXAMPLE** FOR YOU:

DEAR POGS, I CAN'T BELIEVE HOW HAPPY I AM SINCE YOU CAME INTO MY LIFE. YOU ARE TRULY THE BEST FRIEND ANYONE COULD EVER ASK FOR. I WISHED ON A STAR, AND SOON ENOUGH—THERE YOU WERE! YOU NEVER COMPLAIN WHEN I GIVE YOU THE SAME BREAKFAST DAY AFTER DAY. YOU'RE SUCH A GOOD LISTENER. NOW IF ONLY YOU COULD TALK! YOU COULD TELL ME ALL ABOUT YOUR LIFE BEFORE YOU CAME TO LIVE ON MY STREET!

unsung hero

NAME ————————

AGENT ID# ————————

[FULL SECURITY CLEARANCE]

Secret Agent

IMAGINE YOU ARE A SPY OR AN UNDERCOVER AGENT.

Picture your most daring operation. Where has your assignment taken you? What is your task? How do you overcome evil? What do you say just before you defeat your enemy?

• •

HAVING BEEN DISPATCHED TO THE MOST DANGEROUS CITY ON THE PLANET, I EMPLOYED EVERY CLEVER TRICK AT MY DISPOSAL TO TRACK DOWN AND OUTSMART MY TARGET—A CUNNING AND SLIPPERY SCOUNDREL. JUST BEFORE I USED MY FINAL DIRTY DEED TO DEFEAT THIS VILLAIN, I ROARED, "YOU'LL NEVER GET THE BETTER OF ME, YOU VILE BAD GUY!"

———————————— ————————————

———————————— ————————————

———————————— ————————————

———————————— ————————————

———————————— ————————————

———————————— ————————————

WHICH DO YOU LIKE BETTER
⬛ WAFFLES OR PANCAKES? ⬛

OH! I LOVE WAFFLES! WITH BLUEBERRIES, A SCOOP OF ICE CREAM, CRUSHED ALMONDS, COCONUT FLAKES, A SPOONFUL OF WHIPPED CREAM, AND A MARASCHINO CHERRY ON TOP.

⟨ OH, OKAY, NOW YOU ANSWER. ⟩

1 WHICH DO YOU LIKE BETTER—WAFFLES OR PANCAKES?

_____

_____

_____

2 WOULD YOU RATHER HAVE A SMALL PARTY WITH A FEW GOOD FRIENDS, OR A BIG PARTY WITH YOUR FRIENDS, AND THEIR FRIENDS, AND THEIR FRIENDS' FRIENDS?

_____

_____

_____

3 WHEN YOU WATCH AN ACTION MOVIE, DO YOU USUALLY THINK OF YOURSELF AS THE HERO OR THE UNDERDOG?

_____

_____

_____

4 WHAT RULE WOULD YOU BREAK TO HELP A FRIEND?

_____

_____

_____

5 WHEN YOU NEED TO MAKE A BIG DECISION, DO YOU THINK ABOUT THE PROS AND CONS OR GO WITH YOUR GUT REACTION?

_____

_____

_____

6 WHEN TRYING SOMETHING NEW, DO YOU LIKE A LOT OF HELP OR WOULD YOU RATHER DO IT YOURSELF?

_____

_____

_____

7 IF YOU THREW A PARTY, WOULD YOU RATHER HANG OUT WITHOUT A PLAN, GET TOGETHER TO WATCH A MOVIE AND EAT PIZZA, OR PLAN ALL THE ACTIVITIES IN DETAIL BEFORE THE BIG DAY?

_____

_____

_____

8 DO YOU LIKE TO SPEND YOUR FREE TIME A) ALONE READING AND LISTENING TO MUSIC, OR B) WITH FRIENDS PLAYING SPORTS AND GOING TO PARTIES?

_____

_____

_____

 9 IN A GROUP, ARE YOU THE CHATTY ONE OR THE LISTENER?

_____

_____

_____

10 DO YOU LIKE TO BE BUSY OR WOULD YOU RATHER HANG OUT AND RELAX?

_____

_____

_____

11 WHEN YOU HAVE A PROBLEM, DO YOU WORK THROUGH IT YOURSELF OR ASK PEOPLE FOR ADVICE?

_____

_____

_____

12 IF YOU HAD A FIGHT WITH YOUR BEST FRIEND, WHO WOULD APOLOGIZE FIRST?

_____

_____

_____

13 WHEN WAS THE LAST TIME YOU TRIED SOMETHING NEW? WHAT WAS IT?

_____

_____

_____

14 ARE YOU A BATMAN OR A ROBIN?

_____

_____

_____

15 IF YOU COULD HAVE PICKED YOUR OWN NAME, WHAT WOULD YOU HAVE CHOSEN?

_____

_____

_____

BURNING QUESTIONS

LIFE IS A RIDDLE, AND YOU ARE THE DETECTIVE.
Write more questions that help you explore life's mysteries.

Why can't you tickle yourself?

Why doesn't glue stick to the inside of the bottle?

Can you cry underwater?

If you pamper a cow, do you get spoiled milk?

If honesty is the best policy, is dishonesty the second-best policy?

HERE'S LOOKING

AT YOU

People are fascinating, curious, and fun to watch! People watching is a great way to pass the time. It's inspiring to observe the many ways people express their personalities and their fashion sense.

SIT OUTSIDE IN A PUBLIC PLACE AND WATCH PEOPLE. MAKE UP STORIES ABOUT THEM. ARE THEY SPIES? MILLIONAIRES? MAD SCIENTISTS? WHAT ARE THEIR NAMES? WHY ARE THEY THERE? WHAT ARE THEIR RELATIONSHIPS TO EACH OTHER? WHAT DOES THEIR BODY LANGUAGE SAY ABOUT THEM?

HERE'S WHAT I SAW:

WISH LIST

LIST TEN THINGS TO DO THIS YEAR.

Then number them from the most likely to the least likely.

HERE ARE SOME CREATIVE EXAMPLES:

1. JOIN A FLASH MOB
2. HAVE A HOLLYWOOD KISS
3. GO ON A ROAD TRIP
4. ACT IN A PLAY
5. MAKE A HOME MOVIE STARRING MY CAT AND POST IT ONLINE
6. TRY A FOOD I CAN'T PRONOUNCE
7. GET A JOB
8. LEARN TO KNIT BY WATCHING HOW-TO VIDEOS
9. TAKE CARE OF A PLANT
10. SAVE 10 PERCENT OF THE MONEY I EARN

RANKING

RANKING

RANKING

RANKING

RANKING

RANKING

RANKING

RANKING

RANKING

RANKING

THINGS I'M LOVIN'

SO MANY COOL THINGS, SO LITTLE TIME

LIST A BUNCH OF THINGS THAT ARE AWESOME!

BOOKS
I'M LOVIN'

....
....
....
....
....
....
....
....
....
....
....
....
....
....

MOVIES
I'M LOVIN'

....
....
....
....
....
....
....
....
....
....
....
....
....
....

SONGS

I'M LOVIN'

FRIENDS

I'M LOVIN'

SLANG

I'M LOVIN'

FASHION

I'M LOVIN'

WHO?

WHEN?

WHAT?

WHERE?

WHY?

LIST TEN THINGS YOU NEED OR WANT TO DO THIS WEEK.
THEN NUMBER THEM FROM THE MOST IMPORTANT TO THE LEAST IMPORTANT.

HERE ARE SOME EXAMPLES:

DO LAUNDRY
STUDY FOR MATH TEST
BECOME A NEAT FREAK
GET A HAIRCUT
DO YOGA

EAT THREE MEALS A DAY
DESIGN MY FUTURE HOUSE
RELAX MORE
WATCH A MOVIE

FLOSS
TAKE A WALK
READ A BOOK
BAKE COOKIES
SAVE THE ENVIRONMENT

RANKING   DONE

———   -   ◯

———   -   ◯

———   -   ◯

———   -   ◯

———   -   ◯

———   -   ◯

———   -   ◯

———   -   ◯

———   -   ◯

———   -   ◯

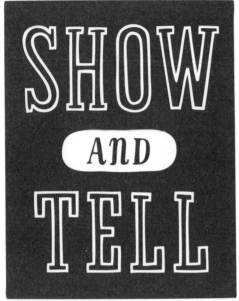

SHOW AND TELL

COLLECT A FEW OF YOUR CHILDHOOD DRAWINGS FROM AROUND THE HOUSE—

from the attic, the basement, or the back of the junk drawer— and make an art exhibit.

THE PURRRFECT PET

WHAT KIND OF PET WOULD YOU RATHER HAVE—A CAT OR A DOG?

Take the Purrrfect Pet Quiz to find out which pet is purrrfect for you!

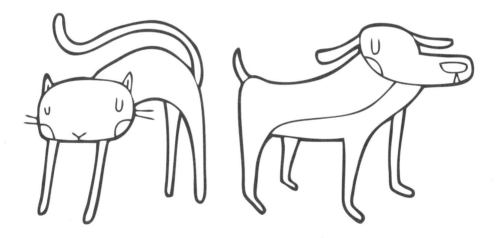

HOW MUCH FREE TIME DO YOU HAVE EACH DAY?

- **a** I have a couple extra hours each day.
- **b** I'm pretty busy with school and other activities. I have about an extra hour each day.
- **c** My days are completely free. I'm on summer break!

DO FURRY ANIMALS MAKE ANYONE IN YOUR HOUSE SNEEZE?

- **a** Not that I know of.
- **b** They make me sneeze, but I can live with that.
- **c** Only my sister/brother, but that doesn't count.

HOW MUCH CAN YOU (OR YOUR PARENTS) SPEND ON YOUR PET EACH MONTH?

a Fifty dollars a month.
b Twenty-five dollars a month.
c I want a pet that doesn't eat and never needs a vet. I'd rather not spend any money on a pet.

HOW ACTIVE ARE YOU?

a I'm very active. Running in the park, walking around the neighborhood—you name it!
b I'm pretty active. I like to walk around the mall once or twice a week.
c I'm the most active person in my virtual world!

HOW LONG WOULD YOU LIKE YOUR PET TO LIVE?

a Eight to twelve years.
b At least ten or fifteen years! I couldn't stand it if my pet died.
c It might not be convenient to take care of a pet next year, so I'd say one year is long enough.

YOU ARE ABOUT TO TAKE A TRIP. WHAT DO YOU SAY TO YOUR PET?

a Oh, my little darling! I'll miss you so much! But Uncle Bob will take good care of you!
b Don't worry! The pet hotel is a really nice place!
c Hey, I'll be back soon, and there's food in the bowl. Why the sad face?

HOW MUCH QUALITY TIME WILL YOU DEVOTE TO YOUR PET?

a I'll spend every waking hour with my pet.
b I can see myself spending an hour or two a day with my pet.
c It depends on my homework, my chores, my friends, and my extra activities. I'll have to play it by ear.

HOW MUCH TIME WILL YOU SPEND TRAINING YOUR PET?

a I can spend two to three hours a day training my pet.
b Maybe thirty minutes a day.
c Wait...what? Pets need training?

PETS CAN BE MESSY CREATURES, AND THEY CAN'T CLEAN UP AFTER THEMSELVES. IS THAT A PROBLEM?

a More fur means more to cuddle!
b I can probably stand to clean up a little fur.
c Pets should clean up after themselves.

WHAT'S YOUR VISION OF YOUR LIFE WITH YOUR PET?

a I'd like to live on a remote island with my pet.
b I'd like a critter to keep me company and appreciate me now and then.
c I really don't like pets much, but since all my friends have one, I thought I might get one, too.

ANSWER KEY

IF YOU ANSWERED A

to most of the questions in the Purrrfect Pet Quiz, a dog is what you need! You seem to have the time, dedication, and energy it takes to meet the needs of a canine companion.

IF YOU ANSWERED B

to most of the questions in the Purrrfect Pet Quiz, a cat might suit you better. A feline friend is a better match for someone with limited free time. Cats need less training than dogs. Because they're independent creatures, cats won't demand so much attention.

IF YOU ANSWERED C

to most of the questions in the Purrrfect Pet Quiz, you should consider waiting to get a dog or a cat. These creatures need lots of love, attention, and training. They can be messy and expensive. If you have a parent who is willing to help care for a pet, maybe you should think about an animal that requires minimal attention such as a turtle, a bird, a fish, or a sloth.

THE WRITING
ON THE WALL

SOME RESEARCHERS BELIEVE

THAT HANDWRITING TELLS A LOT ABOUT AN INDIVIDUAL'S PERSONALITY.
Graphology—the process of analyzing handwriting—may suggest a person's nature.

IF YOUR HANDWRITING SLANTS TO THE RIGHT, YOU ARE SOCIABLE AND OUTGOING. IF IT SLANTS TO THE LEFT, YOU ARE INTROVERTED AND YOU LIKE TO BE ALONE. IF YOUR HANDWRITING IS VERTICAL WITH NO SLANT, YOU ARE PRACTICAL AND CAREFUL ABOUT SHOWING YOUR EMOTIONS. IF YOU WRITE WITH LARGE LETTERS, YOU LIKE THE SPOTLIGHT. IF YOU WRITE WITH SMALL LETTERS, YOU ARE FOCUSED AND SHY.

EXPLORE YOUR HANDWRITING AND YOUR SIGNATURE.

LARGE   small

NEAT   *loopy*

MIRROR   UPSIDE-DOWN

What does your handwriting say about you?

DRAW & DECORATE
YOUR FAVORITE QUOTE
FROM A BLOCKBUSTER MOVIE, TV SERIES, OR BOOK.
Sketch a character or two as well!

KID STUFF

Put baby photo here.

DO YOU EVER WONDER WHAT YOU WERE LIKE AS A YOUNGSTER?

Interview your family members about their memories of you when you were little. Ask what words describe you as a kid.

_____

_____

_____

_____

_____

_____

_____

_____

_____

_____

_____

_____

_____

_____

_____

_____

-THAT-
MAKES
TWO OF US

Imagine what life would be like if you had an identical twin.
(If you are a twin, imagine your life as a triplet.) First, brainstorm
answers to the following questions to spark your imagination. Then turn
the page, and write a story about yourself and your other half.

Who are your main characters? What are they like? Strong? Vulnerable? Extraordinarily cool?

_____

_____

_____

_____

Where does the story take place?

_____

_____

_____

_____

_____

_____

Why do your characters make certain decisions?

_____

_____

_____

_____

_____

_____

Does your story include betrayal? Jealousy? Loyalty? What is the conflict?

_____

_____

_____

_____

_____

_____

What do your main characters learn about themselves? Each other? The world?

_____

_____

_____

_____

_____

_____

Does your story include courage? Hope? Discovery? What event changes everything? What is the resolution?

_____

_____

_____

_____

_____

_____

What's the moral of your story? What do you want the reader to learn?

_____

_____

_____

_____

_____

_____

IT SPEAKS for Itself

SONGS CAN MAKE YOU LAUGH OR CRY.

They can take you back to a special time or make you sing at the top of your lungs. They are your dance partner when you're happy, and they cheer you up when you're blue.

SEARCH OUT SONG LYRICS THAT SING TO YOU

66 _____ 99

66 _____ 99

66 _____ 99

66 _____ 99

66 _____ 99

"   "

"   "

"   "

"   "

"   "

"   "

"   "

"   "

"   "

"   "

"   "

"   "

"   "

"   "

"   "

"   "

LITTLE me

Ask your mom or dad about memorable things you said when you were a kid. What was your first sentence? The funniest thing you said? The smartest? The wackiest? Use them to create your own comic.

Draw your own comic!

RHYME ~OR~ REASON

THERE MUST BE A MILLION KINDS OF POEMS IN THE WORLD WRITTEN FOR A MILLION DIFFERENT REASONS.

What kind of poetry inspires you? Choose a style and write a poem.

ALPHABETICAL

WRITE A POEM THAT BEGINS WITH THE LETTER *A*. THE SECOND LINE BEGINS WITH *B*. EACH LINE BEGINS WITH THE NEXT LETTER OF THE ALPHABET.

AUTOBIOGRAPHICAL

WRITE A POEM ABOUT YOURSELF.

BALLAD

WRITE A POEM THAT RHYMES AND TELLS A REAL-LIFE STORY.

FREE-FORM

WRITE A POEM THAT MAKES SENSE (OR DOESN'T MAKE SENSE), THAT RHYMES (OR DOESN'T RHYME), AND THAT IS TRUE (OR FALSE)— WHATEVER YOU LIKE! YOU CAN PROBABLY GUESS WHY THIS KIND OF POEM IS CALLED FREE-FORM!

FIVE SENSES

WRITE A POEM ABOUT THINGS THAT ARE YOUR FAVORITE COLOR. HOW DO THEY LOOK, SOUND, SMELL, TASTE, AND FEEL?

I WISH

WRITE A POEM OF EIGHT TO TEN LINES. START EACH LINE WITH "I WISH."

PRACTICE MAKES PERFECT

DON'T WORRY ABOUT MISTAKES IN THE PAST. INSTEAD, THINK OF THEM AS A MAP TO A BETTER FUTURE. AFTER ALL, IF YOU DON'T MAKE A MISTAKE, YOU DON'T MAKE ANYTHING!

LOOK BACK OVER YOUR PAST.

Think about a mistake that made you better. Did you learn anything cool about yourself, about other people, or about the situation?

_____

_____

_____

_____

_____

_____

_____

_____

_____

_____

WOULD YOU DO IT DIFFERENTLY NEXT TIME?

_____

_____

_____

_____

_____

_____

_____

_____

_____

_____

_____

_____

-YOU'RE A FINE ONE-
TO TALK

LIST NICE THINGS PEOPLE HAVE SAID ABOUT YOU.

- - - - - - - - - - - - - - - -   - - - - - - - - - - - - - - - -

- - - - - - - - - - - - - - - -   - - - - - - - - - - - - - - - -

- - - - - - - - - - - - - - - -   - - - - - - - - - - - - - - - -

- - - - - - - - - - - - - - - -   - - - - - - - - - - - - - - - -

- - - - - - - - - - - - - - - -   - - - - - - - - - - - - - - - -

- - - - - - - - - - - - - - - -   - - - - - - - - - - - - - - - -

Ever come across a castoff from childhood? A costume or a uniform? A baseball mitt? An old diary? A drawing? A gift? An award, ribbon, or trophy? Go on a scavenger hunt for some of these forgotten things that may be buried in the closet, attic, or basement, and brush off the dust. Fill a shoebox with interesting items from your childhood— things that say, "This is who I am!"

CONJURE UP, COPY,
OR COMPOSE SOME LYRICS.

FIND THEM ON A PLAYLIST, IN YOUR IMAGINATION,

or in the back of your memory!

FINDING

YOUR

FEET

····· · ·· · ···· ···

A OKAY

WHAT WORDS
WOULD YOU USE
TO DESCRIBE
YOURSELF?

Make a list of words you'd use to describe yourself. Then put them into one gigantic sentence of awesomeness (also known as an affirmation)!

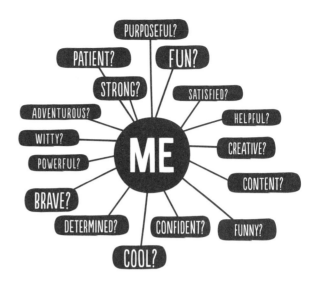

PURPOSEFUL?
PATIENT?
FUN?
STRONG?
SATISFIED?
ADVENTUROUS?
HELPFUL?
WITTY?
CREATIVE?
ME
POWERFUL?
CONTENT?
BRAVE?
DETERMINED?
CONFIDENT?
FUNNY?
COOL?

EXAMPLE

SOME DAY I'LL BE THE COOLEST, MOST CONFIDENT, STRONGEST, BRAVEST, MOST POWERFUL SUPERHERO ON EARTH WITH POWERS THAT WOULD PUT SUPERMAN TO SHAME.

_____

_____

_____

_____

_____

SUPERHERO POWERS

★ ★

OH SUPER!

super badges

INVISIBILITY

NIGHT VISION

SUPER powers

MIND CONTROL

FLIGHT

IF YOU COULD HAVE A SUPERPOWER,

what would it be, and how would you use it?

SUPER DUPER

IF I HAD AN ELASTIC ARM,
I would sneak treats from
the kitchen after midnight!

my power _____

- -
- -
- -
- -
- -

○ SUPER STRENGTH	○ SUPERHUMAN SPEED	○ NIGHT VISION
○ FLIGHT	○ CONTROL OF THE WEATHER	○ FREEZE VISION
○ DESTRUCTIVE ENERGY BEAMS	○ A BIONIC BODY	○ X-RAY VISION
○ FORCE FIELDS	○ TRANSFORMATION	○ IMMORTALITY
○ MAGICAL ARMOR	○ A MAGIC RING	○ REALITY WARPING
○ MIND CONTROL	○ A WISHING LAMP	○ PORTAL CREATION
○ TELEKINESIS	○ REGENERATION	○ ELASTICITY
○ TELEPORTATION	○ DUPLICATION	○ SIZE SHIFTING
○ TIME TRAVEL	○ INVISIBILITY	○ CLAIRVOYANCE

STROKE OF LUCK

People have been predicting the future for centuries by reading palms and tea leaves, looking into a crystal ball, and interpreting tarot cards. Another way to peek into the future is with the help of a paper fortune-teller or whirlybird.

FOLLOW THESE EASY STEPS TO MAKE A SIMPLE FORTUNE-TELLER. THEN, ASK THE TOUGH QUESTIONS AND LET THE FORTUNE-TELLER DECIDE!

1 START WITH A SQUARE PIECE OF PAPER. DECORATE ONE SIDE.

2 WITH THE DECORATED SIDE UP, FOLD IT DIAGONALLY TO CREATE A TRIANGLE. OPEN IT UP AND REPEAT, FOLDING THE PAPER ON THE OTHER DIAGONAL AND THEN UNFOLDING IT.

3 FOLD ALL FOUR CORNERS OF YOUR PAPER INTO THE CENTER SO THE POINTS MEET IN THE MIDDLE.

4 NOW TURN THE FORTUNE-TELLER OVER. FOLD ALL FOUR CORNERS OF THE SQUARE INTO THE CENTER SO THE POINTS MEET IN THE MIDDLE.

[TURN OVER]

5 FOLD THIS IN HALF TO CREATE A RECTANGLE. THEN, FOLD THIS RECTANGLE IN HALF AGAIN TO FORM A SQUARE.

6 NOW THAT YOU'VE CREATED ALL THE CREASES, OPEN YOUR FORTUNE-TELLER, AND WRITE YOUR OWN PROMPTS IN THE FOUR CORNERS TO QUIZ YOUR FRIENDS. (FOLLOW THE EXAMPLE!)

7 FOLLOWING THE EXAMPLE, WRITE EIGHT ANSWERS AND EIGHT NUMBERS.

8 WITH THE DECORATED SIDE UP, REPEAT STEPS 3–5, BUT DON'T FOLD INTO THE FINAL SQUARE. SLIDE YOUR THUMBS AND INDEX FINGERS UNDER THE FLAPS WHERE YOUR PROMPTS ARE WRITTEN. BRING YOUR DIGITS TOGETHER TO SHAPE THE FORTUNE-TELLER.

★ Ask your friend to pick one of the four prompts to come up with a personal question.

★ Spell the question out loud and move the flaps in and out and side to side with each letter.

★ The fortune-teller will reveal four numbers. Ask your friend to pick one.

★ Moving the flaps in the same manner, count out the chosen number.

★ Ask your friend to pick another number. Count again.

★ Ask your friend to pick a third number. Open the flap to reveal the fortune that awaits!

DO I WANT TO...
(eat ice cream for dinner?
go to the moon?
buy a hedgehog?)

5

6

WILL I BE A...
(dog-walker? mom?
dad? freelance
astronaut?
superhero?)

FOR SURE

NOPE

2

3

MAYBE, MAYBE NOT

IT'S HARD TO SAY

YEP!

YES INDEED

1

4

AM I...
(a fun friend? good at
keeping secrets?
going to be famous
some day?)

8

UMM, MAYBE

NUH-UH, NO WAY

7

CAN I...
(graduate from college?
play in a rock band?
learn another
language?)

ALL IN GOOD TIME

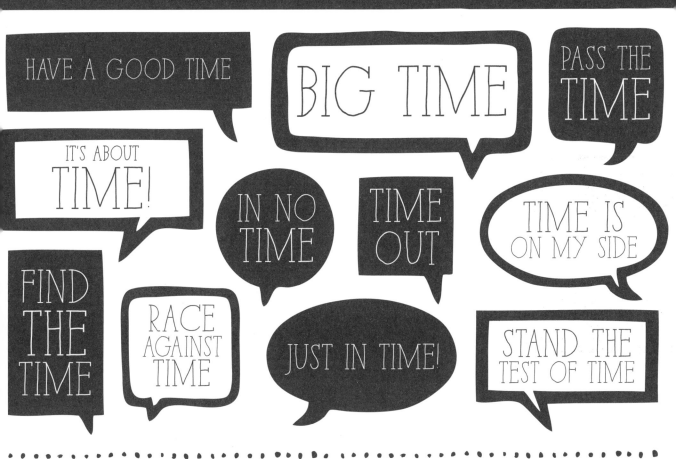

Make a time capsule to preserve objects, store predictions, or stash a letter to your future self. A time capsule can be as simple as a shoebox. It can be sealed with tape, staples, string, or chewing gum, depending on how secure you want it to be. **TODAY:** Save pieces of your modern world. **TEN YEARS FROM NOW:** Open up your past!

CONSIDER THESE QUESTIONS
AS YOU CREATE YOUR CAPSULE:

1

Choose the time period for your capsule. Who will open your capsule? You? Your grandchildren? Some future inhabitants of Earth who have come from a far-off galaxy?

2

Decide where to hide your time capsule. On your closet shelf? Under the bed? In the attic? In the basement? Next to the buried treasure in your backyard? (If you hide it outside, remember to seal it well!)

3

Find a container—a shoebox, a paper-towel roll, or an empty can. How many things will you collect? The size of your continer will depend on how much stuff you want to stow away.

4

Collect the items to put in your time capsule. What items represent you now but may surprise someone in the future? pictures • small change • newspaper or magazine articles • price tags or receipts • letters or postcards • pictures of clothes or hairstyles from your favorite magazine (or of yourself!) toys • packaging from a popular product that will be outdated in a few years food labels • a journal or diary • your favorite things (just not anything you can't stand to part with)

5

Write a description of life today. Write about daily life, current trends, attitudes, and news. Write about the cost of things—a pair of jeans, a gallon of milk, your favorite candy bar. If you plan on opening the time capsule yourself, include a letter to your future self. If someone else will open it, write a letter to that person (keeping in mind that it might just be an alien!).

6

. . . .

SEAL

Seal the time capsule, mark it with the date you intend for it to be opened, and stash it in your secret hiding place for future discovery.

note TO SELF

WHERE WILL YOUR FUTURE LEAD YOU?

Write a letter to your future self. What advice do you have? Any words of wisdom or caution for the you of the future?

YOU KNOW I'M YOUR BIGGEST FAN! YOU'RE SUPER FUNNY, BUT SOMETIMES YOU'RE A LITTLE TOO SENSITIVE! YOU NEED TO BE TOUGHER IF YOU'RE GOING TO CONQUER MISSION IMPOSSIBLE. I WANT TO HELP YOU BE THE COOLEST *YOU* EVER. OBVIOUSLY, WE'RE IN THIS TOGETHER!

As you write,
think about these

QUESTIONS

☐ How do you see yourself
in the future?

- - - - - - - - - - - - - - - - - -
- - - - - - - - - - - - - - - - - -
- - - - - - - - - - - - - - - - - -
- - - - - - - - - - - - - - - - - -

☐ What are your goals, and why
are they important to you?

- - - - - - - - - - - - - - - - - -
- - - - - - - - - - - - - - - - - -
- - - - - - - - - - - - - - - - - -
- - - - - - - - - - - - - - - - - -

☐ What awesome qualities do
you have that will help?

- - - - - - - - - - - - - - - - - -
- - - - - - - - - - - - - - - - - -
- - - - - - - - - - - - - - - - - -
- - - - - - - - - - - - - - - - - -

☐ How strongly do you believe in yourself
and your ability to hit the mark?

- - - - - - - - - - - - - - - - - -
- - - - - - - - - - - - - - - - - -
- - - - - - - - - - - - - - - - - -
- - - - - - - - - - - - - - - - - -

☐ What fears do you face?
How will you tackle them?

- - - - - - - - - - - - - - - - - -
- - - - - - - - - - - - - - - - - -
- - - - - - - - - - - - - - - - - -
- - - - - - - - - - - - - - - - - -

☐ How will you continue to encourage
yourself if times get tough?

- - - - - - - - - - - - - - - - - -
- - - - - - - - - - - - - - - - - -
- - - - - - - - - - - - - - - - - -
- - - - - - - - - - - - - - - - - -

☐ Who else will be there to
inspire you?

- - - - - - - - - - - - - - - - - -
- - - - - - - - - - - - - - - - - -
- - - - - - - - - - - - - - - - - -
- - - - - - - - - - - - - - - - - -

☐ What does your life
story look like?

- - - - - - - - - - - - - - - - - -
- - - - - - - - - - - - - - - - - -
- - - - - - - - - - - - - - - - - -
- - - - - - - - - - - - - - - - - -

note TO SELF

○

○

○

Continue...

note TO SELF

SAVE IT FOR A RAINY DAY

WHAT WOULD YOU DO
IF YOU HAD A HUNDRED DOLLARS?

A THOUSAND DOLLARS?
A MILLION DOLLARS? WHEN
YOU'RE SAVING MONEY,
EVERY PENNY COUNTS.

MAKE A LIST OF THINGS
YOU WOULD BUY OR DO IF
YOU HAD THE MONEY.

BUY A NEW CELL PHONE

TRAVEL AROUND THE WORLD IN MY OWN YACHT

BUILD A LABORATORY ON MARS

TWIST OF FATE

DO YOU EVER WONDER WHAT YOUR FUTURE HOLDS?

Will you marry? How many children will you have? What kind of car will you drive? Will you live in a mansion, an apartment, a shack, or a house? Play the game of M.A.S.H. to find out. If you don't like the results, start over!

M.A.S.H. is a game you play with a friend. Ask your friend to do the following:

1. Pick two people you like and two you dislike. Write their names in the template.

2. Next, write two cities you like and two you dislike.

3. Write the number of kids you can imagine having (two reasonable numbers) and the number of kids you can't imagine having (two ridiculous numbers).

4. Write the names of two cars you dream of driving and two you'd be embarrassed to drive.

5. Pick a number between 2 and 10.

Now, count from the first item on the list to the last (including the letters M.A.S.H., which stand for Mansion, Apartment, Shack, and House), crossing out each item when you reach your friend's number. Continue counting from there, eliminating items in the same way until you have paired your friend with only one home, one marriage candidate, one city, one number of kids, and a car. The sample will help you out.

M.A.S.H.

Kiran ~~Portland~~
~~Finn~~ ~~Seattle~~
~~Sara~~ Kilmore
~~Bryanna~~ Tuba City

┼ Mini
3 ~~Bentley~~
12 ~~Gremlin~~
1,369 El Camino

_____

M.A.S.H.

·············· ··············
·············· ··············
·············· ··············
·············· ··············

·············· ··············
·············· ··············
·············· ··············
·············· ··············

_____

M.A.S.H.

·············· ··············
·············· ··············
·············· ··············
·············· ··············

·············· ··············
·············· ··············
·············· ··············
·············· ··············

_____

M.A.S.H.

·············· ··············
·············· ··············
·············· ··············
·············· ··············

·············· ··············
·············· ··············
·············· ··············
·············· ··············

_____

M.A.S.H.

·············· ··············
·············· ··············
·············· ··············
·············· ··············

·············· ··············
·············· ··············
·············· ··············
·············· ··············

_____

M.A.S.H.

·············· ··············
·············· ··············
·············· ··············
·············· ··············

·············· ··············
·············· ··············
·············· ··············
·············· ··············

_____

A better ME

/Im'prüvmənt/

Make a pledge to improve yourself, and set some small goals along the way. Use one cool new vocabulary word every day from the following list. Then make up your own list.

RUBBLE

There was a *noxious* odor coming from his locker

HUMANE

ADVOCATE

SPONTANEOUS

NOXIOUS

TEDIOUS

TALISMAN

IMPERATIVE

In her pocket she carried his love n like a *talisman*

ECCENTRIC

LUCRATIV

FACE YOUR FEARS

FOR ONE WEEK, NOTICE WHAT MAKES YOU FEEL NERVOUS OR NEGATIVE. WRITE THINGS DOWN, SCRIBBLE IN YOUR NOTEPAD, OR TAKE NOTES ON YOUR PHONE, AND THEN CHALLENGE YOUR THINKING BY ASKING YOURSELF A FEW QUESTIONS.

NEGATIVE THOUGHT:

I'M SO SCARED THAT MY TEACHER WILL CALL ON ME IN CLASS, AND I WON'T KNOW THE ANSWER. SHE'LL GET MAD, AND I'LL LOOK STUPID!

WHAT COULD YOU DO TO REDUCE YOUR FEAR IN THIS SITUATION?

I GUESS I COULD JUST SAY, "I'M SORRY, BUT I'M NOT SURE." THEN THE TEACHER WOULD ASK ANOTHER STUDENT, AND I'D BE OFF THE HOOK.

WHAT WOULD YOU SAY TO A FRIEND WHO WAS NERVOUS ABOUT THE SAME THING?

I WOULD PROBABLY SAY, "YOU KNOW THE RIGHT ANSWER NINE TIMES OUT OF TEN. IT'S OK IF YOU DON'T KNOW THE ANSWER ALL THE TIME!"

POSITIVE THOUGHT:

ACTUALLY, OUR TEACHER DOESN'T EXPECT PERFECTION. SHE JUST WANTS US TO DO OUR BEST.

NEGATIVE THOUGHT:

_____

WHAT COULD YOU DO TO REDUCE YOUR FEAR IN THIS SITUATION?

_____

WHAT WOULD YOU SAY TO A FRIEND WHO WAS NERVOUS ABOUT THE SAME THING?

_____

POSITIVE THOUGHT:

_____

. . ..

NEGATIVE THOUGHT:

_____

WHAT COULD YOU DO TO REDUCE YOUR FEAR IN THIS SITUATION?

_____

WHAT WOULD YOU SAY TO A FRIEND WHO WAS NERVOUS ABOUT THE SAME THING?

_____

POSITIVE THOUGHT:

_____

DREAM UP, DRAW &
DECORATE AMAZING LINES OF POETRY—
RHYMING, LIMERICK, OR FREE-FORM—
any style will do!

SURVEY SAYS

DO YOU EVER WONDER HOW SIMILAR YOU AND YOUR BFF REALLY ARE?

Do you think alike? Do you have the same goals and dreams? Are you attracted to the same type? How about a little Q&A?

(YOU'VE GOT IT! THAT'S QUESTION AND ANSWER!)

WHAT FADS HAVE YOU LOVED? HATED?

 Skinny jeans—love 'em! Oh, but I've always hated neon!

1. If you were talking in
your sleep, what are you
afraid you would say?

YOU

BFF

2. Do you know any
jokes by heart?

YOU

BFF

3. How long does it take
you to get ready in the
morning?

YOU

BFF

4. Where do you buy most
of your clothes?

YOU

BFF

5. If you were from another country, where would you want to be from?

YOU _____
_____
_____

BFF _____
_____
_____

6. What food is disgusting?

YOU _____
_____
_____

BFF _____
_____
_____

7. What trends make you LOL?

YOU _____
_____
_____

BFF _____
_____
_____

8. What songs always get stuck in your head?

YOU _____
_____
_____

BFF _____
_____
_____

9. What is the best advice that you ever received?

YOU
_____
_____
_____

BFF
_____
_____
_____

10. What's the best advice that you wish you had taken?

YOU
_____
_____
_____

BFF
_____
_____
_____

11. Has anyone told you that you look like someone famous?

YOU
_____
_____
_____

BFF
_____
_____
_____

12. When you were a kid, what vegetables did you leave on your plate?

YOU
_____
_____
_____

BFF
_____
_____
_____

13. What was your favorite Halloween costume?

YOU
_____
_____
_____

BFF
_____
_____
_____

14. If you were a super-hero, who would you be?

YOU
_____
_____
_____

BFF
_____
_____
_____

15. Silver or gold?

YOU
_____
_____
_____

BFF
_____
_____
_____

16. Blond or brunette?

YOU
_____
_____
_____

BFF
_____
_____
_____

17. What do you want to be doing in ten years?

YOU
_____
_____
_____

BFF
_____
_____
_____

18. What feature do you usually notice first? Eyes? Smile? Something else?

YOU
_____
_____
_____

BFF
_____
_____
_____

19. Have you ever run away from home?

YOU
_____
_____
_____

BFF
_____
_____
_____

20. Describe your first crush.

YOU
_____
_____
_____

BFF
_____
_____
_____

21. What songs bring back childhood memories?

YOU

BFF

22. Have you ever broken a bone or had an operation?

YOU

BFF

23. Have you ever had a nickname that you liked? How about hated?

YOU

BFF

24. Have you ever cheated on a test?

YOU

BFF

A NOD'S
AS GOOD AS A WINK

Body language says a lot about a person. A wink, a scowl, a nod—all of these give hints about your mood, suggest your attitude, and reveal your personality. What can you convey with body language alone?

PLAY A NONSENSE GAME WITH A FRIEND. TALK TO EACH OTHER FOR FIVE OR TEN MINUTES IN A MADE-UP LANGUAGE. CHANGE YOUR TONE OF VOICE AND YOUR BODY LANGUAGE TO GET YOUR MESSAGE ACROSS. RAISE AN EYEBROW. PUT YOUR HANDS ON YOUR HIPS. SKIP. HOW MANY MOODS CAN YOU COMMUNICATE?

SPOILED ROTTEN

FEEL LIKE PAMPERING A FRIEND FOR A SPECIAL OCCASION—OR FOR NO REASON AT ALL? PRESENT AN ACTION COUPON AS A PLEDGE TO SPOIL YOUR FRIEND ROTTEN.

GIVE ME THIS COUPON WHEN YOU FEEL LIKE A FREE
ICE-CREAM CONE
ICE CREAM

THIS COUPON IS GOOD FOR SOME
FREE ADVICE
WHEN YOU'RE STUCK BETWEEN A ROCK AND A HARD PLACE!
★ ★ ★ ★ ★ ★ ★ ★ ★
FREE ADVICE

≫ THIS ≪
COUPON
IS GOOD FOR ONE BATCH OF HOMEMADE COOKIES!

WHEN YOU REDEEM THIS COUPON
I'LL HELP YOU WITH YOUR HOMEWORK!
YOUR HOMEWORK

THIS COUPON IS GOOD FOR ONE
PEP TALK
WHEN YOU'RE DOWN!

THIS COUPON IS GOOD FOR
★ A TRIP TO THE MOVIES! ★
MOVIE
CLIP THIS COUPON HERE

CREATE ONE OF YOUR OWN!
COUPON

THIS COUPON
IS GOOD FOR A
SPECIAL LUNCH
ON ME!
GOOD LUNCH

IT'S A LONG STORY

TWO HEADS ARE BETTER THAN ONE!

Work with a friend or two to write a story. Use the example first line here, or start your story by writing your own first line. Then ask a friend to add the next line. Take turns adding to the story until you have a long story.

No one would ever have believed me if I had told them what really happened that day.

_____

_____

_____

_____

_____

_____

_____

_____

_____

_____ Continue...

KEEP ME POSTED

Most of us are so busy texting, chatting, messaging, and posting online that we rarely think about connecting the old-fashioned way—with pen (or pencil, of course) and paper! Create a postcard for a friend and send it to them by snail mail!

DREAM UP, DRAW & DECORATE

this postcard with your favorite quote from someone who inspires you.

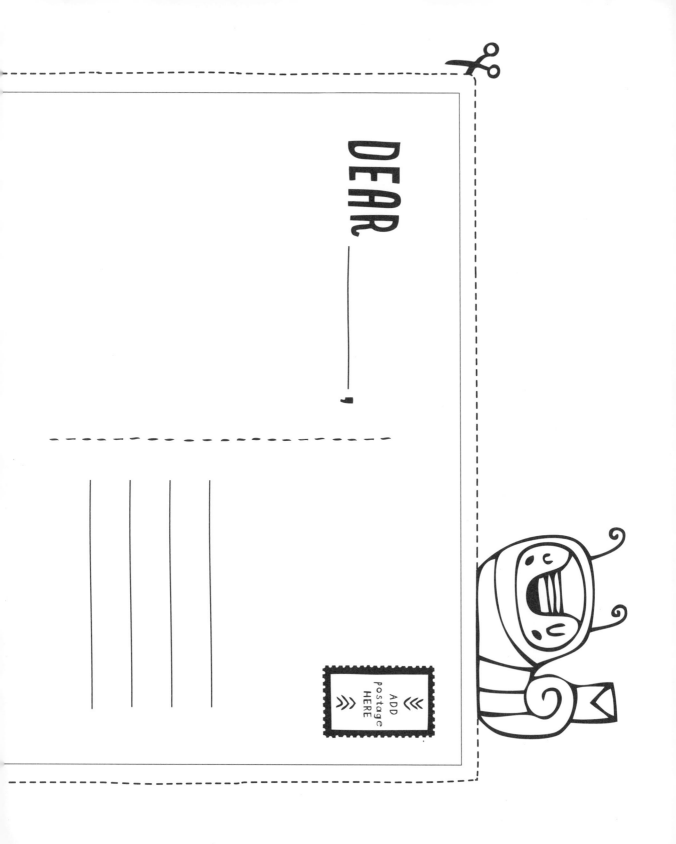

DEAR

_____,

ADD
postage
HERE

YOUR SECRET'S SAFE WITH ME

With some friends, we talk about the weather.
With others, we share even classified information.
List friends you would trust with your deepest secrets.

_____   _____

_____   _____

_____   _____

_____   _____

_____   _____

_____   _____

THE BIG PICTURE

DRAW. PAINT. PORTRAY. OUTLINE. TRACE. SKETCH.

Using a pencil, a crayon, or paint, create a self-portrait and portraits of three friends.

RULE OF THUMB

IMAGINE THIS:

You are the principal of your school, and your best friend is the vice principal. What rules would you get rid of? What new rules would you dream up? What else would you change about your school?

STUPID OLD RULES:

COOL NEW RULES:

OTHER CHANGES:

ALLOW ME

WE'VE ALL DONE LITTLE THINGS TO HELP OUR FRIENDS.

THOSE ACTS OF KINDNESS MAKE US FEEL GOOD ABOUT OURSELVES, TOO! MAKE A LIST OF THINGS YOU'VE DONE FOR YOUR FRIENDS THAT MAKE YOU PROUD.

EXAMPLES

✳ Shared my lunch with a friend.

✳ Secretly tucked cute little notes into my friend's bag, book, or coat pocket.

✳ Wrote my friend's homework when she broke her hand.

✳ Bought my friend ten packs of her favorite gum when she was down.

your favorite quote!

DREAM UP, DRAW &
DECORATE YOUR FAVORITE QUOTE
FROM A COMEDIAN OR PERSONAL HERO—SOMEONE WHO INSPIRES YOU.

Search books, magazines, or online videos for inspiration!

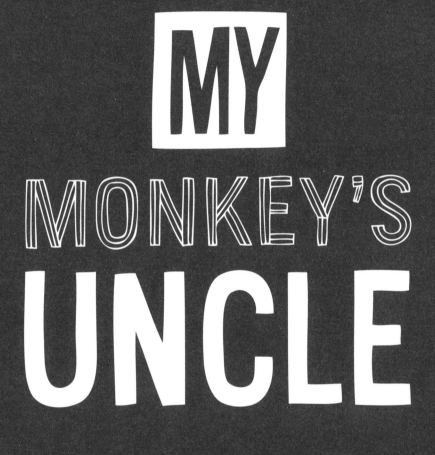

MY MONKEY'S UNCLE

A NEW LEASE ON LIFE

IMAGINE YOU LIVED IN VERY DIFFERENT CIRCUMSTANCES—

as an undercover spy with multiple high-tech gadgets to help bring mysteries to light, or on a deserted island with only your courage and wit to guide you. What would your life be like? Imagine the best-case and worst-case scenarios.

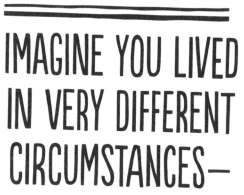

KEY

- - - - - LIFE
▬▬▬ FRIENDS
═══ HOME
╫╫╫╫ FAMILY
⚬── SCHOOL

Where would you live? In a distant country? In the tropics? Wonderland? Camelot?

_____   _____
_____   _____
_____   _____
_____   _____

What would your family be like? Would you have brothers and sisters? How many? Would they be younger or older? Would you already have nieces and nephews? Would any of your brothers and sisters be newborn babies? Suppose you had ten or twelve siblings. Would they all live at home?

_____   _____
_____   _____
_____   _____
_____   _____
_____   _____

What would your school be like? Would it be a public, private, or home school? Maybe your school would have dirt floors. Or maybe it wouldn't have heat or air-conditioning. What crazy subjects would you study?

_____   _____
_____   _____
_____   _____
_____   _____

FOOD FOR THOUGHT

DO YOU EVER GET TO THE END OF THE DAY AND REALIZE ALL YOU'VE EATEN IS JUNK FOOD?

Sometimes being aware of your bad habits is enough to make you change them.

KEEP A DAILY RECORD OF WHAT YOU AND YOUR FAMILY EAT FOR BREAKFAST, LUNCH, DINNER, AND SNACKS. REVIEW IT AFTER A WEEK. ARE THERE THINGS THAT YOU'D LIKE TO CHANGE? ARE THERE WAYS THAT YOU CAN HELP WITH MEAL PLANNING?

BREAKFAST
· · · · · · · · · · · · · ·
{DAY —— }

· · · · · · · · · · · · · ·
{DAY —— }

· · · · · · · · · · · · · ·
{DAY —— }

· · · · · · · · · · · · · ·
{DAY —— }

LUNCH
· · · · · · · · · · · · · ·
{DAY —— }

· · · · · · · · · · · · · ·
{DAY —— }

· · · · · · · · · · · · · ·
{DAY —— }

· · · · · · · · · · · · · ·
{DAY —— }

DINNER
· · · · · · · · · · · · · ·
{DAY —— }

· · · · · · · · · · · · · ·
{DAY —— }

· · · · · · · · · · · · · ·
{DAY —— }

· · · · · · · · · · · · · ·
{DAY —— }

SNACKS
· · · · · · · · · · · · · ·
{DAY —— }

· · · · · · · · · · · · · ·
{DAY —— }

· · · · · · · · · · · · · ·
{DAY —— }

· · · · · · · · · · · · · ·
{DAY —— }

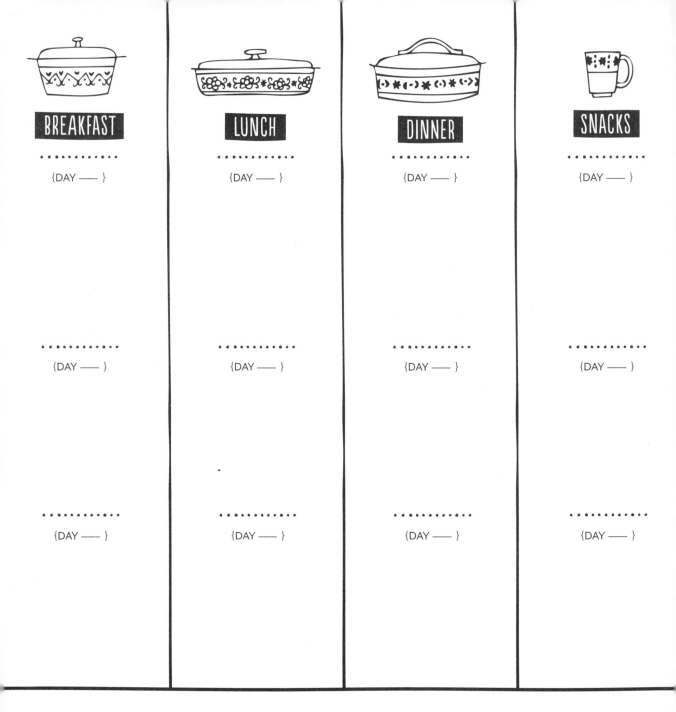

BREAKFAST

· · · · · · · · · · · ·
{DAY —— }

· · · · · · · · · · · ·
{DAY —— }

· · · · · · · · · · · ·
{DAY —— }

LUNCH

· · · · · · · · · · · ·
{DAY —— }

· · · · · · · · · · · ·
{DAY —— }

· · · · · · · · · · · ·
{DAY —— }

DINNER

· · · · · · · · · · · ·
{DAY —— }

· · · · · · · · · · · ·
{DAY —— }

· · · · · · · · · · · ·
{DAY —— }

SNACKS

· · · · · · · · · · · ·
{DAY —— }

· · · · · · · · · · · ·
{DAY —— }

· · · · · · · · · · · ·
{DAY —— }

What did you learn? What changes will you make?

_____

_____

_____

BRING DOWN THE HOUSE!

PLAY A GIG! TOOT YOUR OWN HORN!
CALL THE TUNE!
STRIKE A CHORD!

Gather up a few sound-making devices from around the house (pots & pans, buckets & spoons). Hand them out to your family, and perform an impromptu concert!

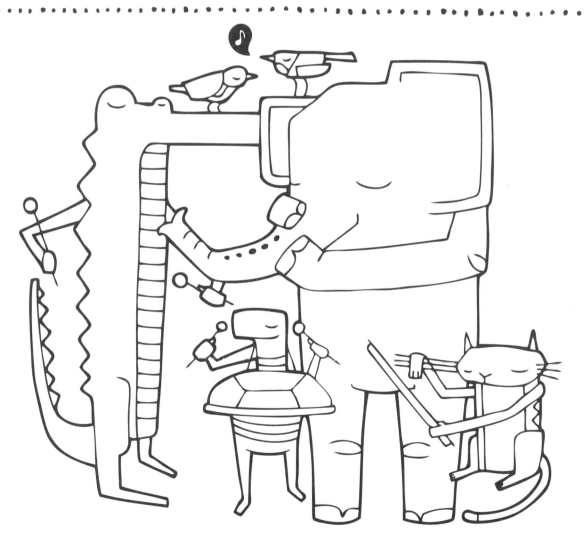

➤ Hey, after your concert, this would be a perfect page for coloring!

ON YOUR MARK, GET SET, GO

>>>>>>>>>>>>>>>>>>>

DO YOU DREAM OF BEING A WORLD TRAVELER? IF YOU WON AN
ALL-EXPENSES-PAID FAMILY VACATION, WHERE WOULD YOU GO?
THE SKY'S THE LIMIT!

I would love to see Big Ben in England.

I would definitely go to the Great Wall of China.

The Colosseum in Italy would be a dream come true!

I've always dreamed of the Taj Mahal in India.

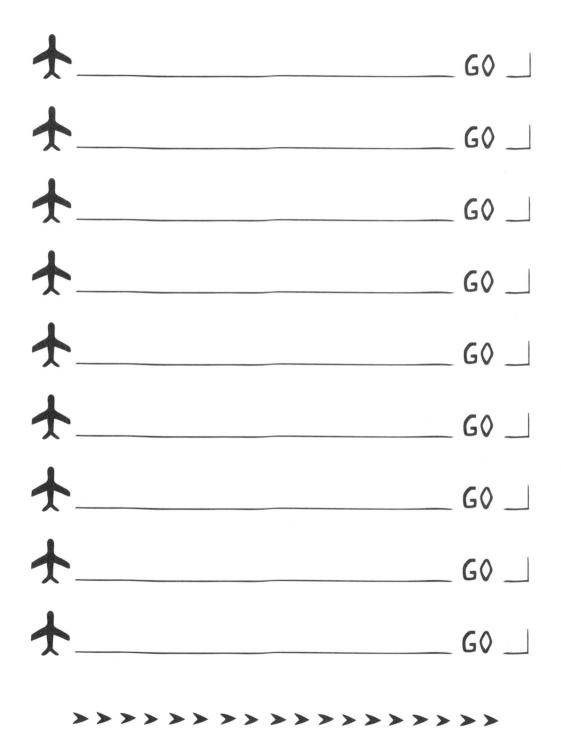

✈ _____ GO ⌐

✈ _____ GO ⌐

✈ _____ GO ⌐

✈ _____ GO ⌐

✈ _____ GO ⌐

✈ _____ GO ⌐

✈ _____ GO ⌐

✈ _____ GO ⌐

✈ _____ GO ⌐

>>>>>>>>>>>>>>>>>>>>>>>>>>

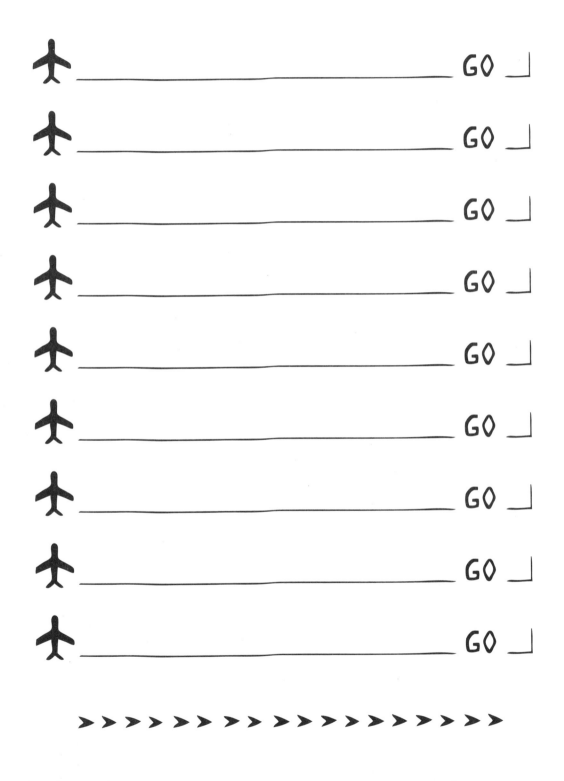

✈ _____ GO ⌋

✈ _____ GO ⌋

✈ _____ GO ⌋

✈ _____ GO ⌋

✈ _____ GO ⌋

✈ _____ GO ⌋

✈ _____ GO ⌋

✈ _____ GO ⌋

✈ _____ GO ⌋

>>>>>>>>>>>>>>>>>>>>>>

A *Little* ELBOW GREASE

FEEL LIKE DOING SOMETHING NICE AROUND THE HOUSE? PRESENT AN ACTION COUPON AS A PLEDGE TO HELP YOUR MOM OR DAD WITH WEEKLY CHORES.

SAVE

THIS COUPON IS GOOD FOR TAKING OUT THE GARBAGE. REALLY! NO WHINING. NO COMPLAINING.

TAKING GARBAGE

WHEN YOU REDEEM THIS COUPON,

I'LL CLEAN MY ROOM!

ROOM CLEANING

{CLIP HERE TO SAVE!}

CLIP

WHEN YOU REDEEM THIS COUPON, I'LL DO MY HOMEWORK WITHOUT COMPLAINING—BEFORE O-DARK-THIRTY!

{CLIP HERE TO SAVE!}

{CLIP HERE TO SAVE!}

WHEN YOU REDEEM THIS **COUPON**

WASH DISHES

I'LL WASH THE DISHES AFTER DINNER—EVEN THE POTS & PANS!

MOST VALUABLE COUPON TO DATE!

≫ WHEN YOU ≪

REDEEM

HOUSE CLEANING

★ THIS COUPON, I'LL SWEEP OR VACUUM THE WHOLE HOUSE!

WHEN YOU REDEEM THIS COUPON,

I'LL MOW THE LAWN

LAWN MOWING

NO WHINING, REALLY!

ALL ABOUT SAVINGS

THIS COUPON IS GOOD FOR A CAR WASH. I'LL DO IT BY HAND!

HAND CAR WASH

{CLIP HERE TO SAVE!}

{CREATE YOUR OWN VALUE COUPON!}

VOUCHER

MEMORY LANE

THERE'S ALWAYS THAT ONE SONG THAT BRINGS BACK MEMORIES.

What song reminds you of a special person, a memorable place, or an unforgettable time? Ask your mom, your dad, your brothers and sisters, your aunts and uncles, cousins, and cousins' monkey's brother's uncle. That ought to cover it!

SCAREDY CAT

EVERYONE IS AFRAID OF SOMETHING.

Interview your family members to find out about their phobias.

· ·

WHAT ABOUT THIS ONE?

hip·po·pot·o·mon·stro·ses·qui·ped·a·lio·pho·bi·a:
fear of long words

· ·

Or some of these?

☐ heights   ☐ speaking in public
☐ failure   ☐ creepy, crawly things
☐ clowns   ☐ small spaces

family member	phobia

NAME: Granny
BORN: Bellyside Hill, UK

NAME: Forefather
BORN: Boggy Bottom, UK

NAME: Uncle
BORN: Pity Me, England

NAME: Auntie
BORN: Eek, AK

NAME: Dad
BORN: Nether Wallop, England

NAME: Mom
BORN: Bird-in-Hand, PA

NAME: Cousin
LANGUAGE: Mumbo Jumbo
BORN: Boring, OR

NAME: Cousin
LANGUAGE: Pig Latin
BORN: Soda Springs, CA

NAME: Cousin
LANGUAGE: Babble
BORN: Soda Springs, CA

NAME: Sibling
LANGUAGE: Gobbledygook
BORN: Zigzag, OR

NAME: Sibling
LANGUAGE: Gobbledygook
BORN: Zigzag, OR

IT RUNS IN THE FAMILY

A FAMILY TREE CAN BE USED TO TRACE CONNECTIONS AMONG FAMILY MEMBERS, SHOWCASE FUN OR SILLY FAMILY PHOTOS, AND RECORD CRAZY ADVENTURES, MEMOIRS, LEGENDS, AND MYTHS CONNECTED TO YOUR FAMILY.

1 Collect the names of family members. (You can include additional information if you have it—birth dates, birthplaces, death dates, death places, languages, spiritual beliefs, and level of education of relatives.)

2 Using the illustration as a guide, draw your own family tree. Start with your immediate family. Don't forget to include yourself.

3 Add notes, stories, and facts that you've learned along the way.

SAYS WHO?

EVERY GENERATION COOKS UP NEW SLANG TERMS.

THE EXPRESSIONS WE USE SHOW THAT WE BELONG TO A COMMON GROUP OR COMMUNITY.

Draw a line to match the expressions with their meanings.

Listen to your relatives from different generations—grandparents, aunts and uncles, cousins. Which expressions do they use? If you're not sure about the slang that was popular during a certain decade, ask relatives who have heard slang come and go over the years!

1920s

airtight	very attractive
copacetic	unlikable person
dough	influential person
fire extinguisher	excellent, first-rate
flat tire	money
jalopy	chaperone
pill	dull, disappointing date
big cheese	old car

1930s

swell	behind in one's studies
I'll be a monkey's uncle	men's underwear
gig	I agree
skivvies	attractive person
behind the grind	cool, great
you and me both	I don't believe it
pip	job

1940s

blockbuster	excellent, fashionable, or enjoyable
keeping up with the Joneses	someone's creative idea
cool	kiss
smooch	huge success
greenback	competing to own as much stuff
brainchild	as the neighbors
	dollar

1950s

Big Brother	money
boss	doing well
bread	someone of authority who
chariot	is monitoring you
cookin'	great place or thing
earthbound	hello
fat city	car
hey, bean	reliable
	fantastic

1960s

groovy	cool, excellent, fashionable, amazing
hippie	young adult who rebelled against established culture and criticized middle-class values
the Man	person of authority; a group in power
neat	nice; appealing
fink	tattletale
rags	clothes
solid	Okay or all right

1970s

catch you on the flip side	amazing
dig it	cope with problems
far out	that's surprising
baloney	see you later
keep on truckin'	to like or understand something
right on	that's not true
hotdog	I agree with you

1980s

chillin'	great; difficult and dangerous
dweeb	expensive, classic fashion style
fly	awesome
gag me with a spoon	relaxing
gnarly	cool
preppy	nerd, a geek, someone who is not cool
tubular	lazy person
couch potato	disgusting

1990s

dis	dollars
it's all good	freaking out
my bad	show disrespect
phat	what's up
wassup	everything's fine
word	my fault
beans	yes; I agree
trippin'	excellent, first-rate

2000s

bling	laughing out loud
sketchy	flashy jewelry
peeps	rolling on the floor laughing
rents	unsafe or questionable
sweet	you only live once
YOLO	beyond cool
LOL	friends
ROFL	parents

DREAM UP, DRAW &
DECORATE A MEMORABLE LINE FROM
A SONG FROM YOUR CHILDHOOD. THINK ABOUT CAMPFIRE TUNES,
nursery rhymes, or road-trip songs!

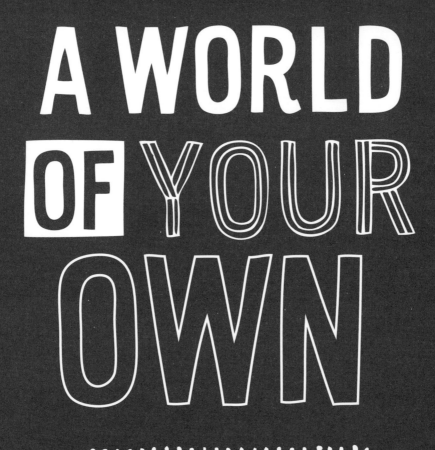

LOST AND FOUND

HAVE YOU EVER FOUND AN UNUSUAL COIN ON THE STREET? A GLOVE? A LEAF SHAPED LIKE A HEART? A SHOE?

Collect a handful of objects from around the neighborhood: a feather, a seed, a rock, a discarded newspaper. When you're finished collecting, step back, and take a look at all of your amazing finds. Create an exhibit by sketching your collection on the next page.

FOUND OBJECTS FROM MY NEIGHBORHOOD

FINDERS KEEPERS

LOOK AT THE NEXT PAGE

HOW MANY CUTE, LITTLE THINGS & CREATURES CAN YOU SPOT?

- - - - - - - - - - - - - - - - -

wishboat hats _ _ _ _   owls _ _ _ _
berries _ _ _ _   umbrellas _ _ _ _
clouds _ _ _ _   mushrooms _ _ _ _
foxes _ _ _ _   raindrops _ _ _ _
paper airplanes _ _ _ _   acorns _ _ _ _
leaves _ _ _ _   elephants _ _ _ _
sparrows _ _ _ _   badgers _ _ _ _
bumblebees _ _ _ _

13 wishboat hats, 33 berries, 4 clouds, 4 foxes, 4 paper airplanes, 32 leaves,
11 sparrows, 20 bumblebees, 5 owls, 6 umbrellas, 34 mushrooms, 27 raindrops,
8 acorns, 1 elephant, 1 badger

FINDERS KEEPERS

ALL SMILES

SMILING MAKES YOU FEEL GOOD.

It makes others feel good, too. Smiling creates a sense of trust between people and cheers people up when they're down.

• •

TODAY, SMILE AT EVERYONE YOU SEE—EVEN GRUMPY PEOPLE—AND COUNT HOW MANY SMILES YOU GET BACK.

GUFFAW   BEAM   SMIRK   CHUCKLE   CHORTLE

SNICKER   GRIN   CACKLE   GIGGLE   LAUGH

A HELPING HAND

FEEL LIKE DOING GOOD IN THE COMMUNITY? PRESENT AN ACTION COUPON TO SOMEONE WHO WILL HELP KEEP YOU ON TASK. ASK FOR SOME SUPPORT IN FOLLOWING THROUGH ON YOUR PLEDGE.

THIS IS MY PLEDGE:

GATHER OLD TOYS & DELIVER THEM TO A CHARITY.

I'VE CHOSEN YOU AS MY CHEERLEADER. KEEP ME ON TASK!

OLD TOYS

X

THIS IS MY PLEDGE:

HELP A NEIGHBOR WITH YARD WORK OR CHORES.

I'VE CHOSEN YOU AS MY CHEERLEADER. KEEP ME ON TASK!

{CREATE A PLEDGE OF YOUR OWN!}

X

THIS IS MY PLEDGE:

TAKE THE NEIGHBOR'S DOG FOR A WALK.

WALK THE DOG

I'VE CHOSEN YOU AS MY CHEERLEADER. KEEP ME ON TASK!

X

THIS IS MY PLEDGE:

TAKE CANNED FOOD TO A HOMELESS SHELTER.

I'VE CHOSEN YOU AS MY CHEERLEADER. KEEP ME ON TASK!

TOMATOES SOUP BEANS FOR SOUP DELICIOUS

CANNED FOOD

THIS IS MY PLEDGE:

VOLUNTEER AT A NURSING HOME.

{OR OTHER CHARITY.}

I'VE CHOSEN YOU AS MY CHEERLEADER. KEEP ME ON TASK!

X

THIS IS MY PLEDGE:

HELP A NEIGHBOR BY ★ BABYSITTING.

I'VE CHOSEN YOU AS MY CHEERLEADER. KEEP ME ON TASK!

X

BABYSITTING

THIS IS MY PLEDGE:

GATHER OLD BOOKS & DONATE THEM TO THE LIBRARY.

ALICE IN WONDERLAND RED RIDING HOOD BLACK BEAUTY

I'VE CHOSEN YOU AS MY CHEERLEADER. KEEP ME ON TASK!

X

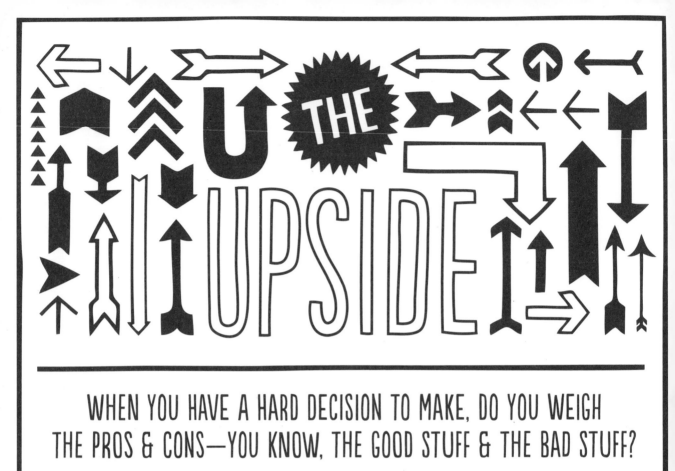

THE UPSIDE

WHEN YOU HAVE A HARD DECISION TO MAKE, DO YOU WEIGH THE PROS & CONS—YOU KNOW, THE GOOD STUFF & THE BAD STUFF?

QUESTION: Should I have a slumber party with friends instead of studying for tomorrow's test?

PROS ▲

- ☐ Have awesome time with friends
- ☐ Sneak treats at midnight
- ☐ Stay up all night
- ☐ Watch a cool movie

CONS ▼

- ☐ Fail the test
- ☐ Disappoint teacher
- ☐ Upset parents
- ☐ Get worst score in class

DO YOU HAVE DECISIONS THAT HAVE BEEN BUGGING YOU?

This is my
QUESTION: _____

PROS	CONS

This is my
QUESTION:

PROS ▲

CONS ▼

This is my
QUESTION: --

PROS ▲	CONS ▼

This is my
QUESTION: --

PROS ▲	CONS ▼

TAKE WHAT YOU NEED:

{ WHY LEAVE FORTUNE TO CHANCE? TODAY, PICK YOUR OWN LUCK! }

OR SLIP SOME LUCK INTO A FRIEND'S POCKET

➤ Post this somewhere for your world to see!

THINK FOR YOURSELF.

NOTHING VENTURED, NOTHING GAINED.

YOU HAVE A SECRET ADMIRER.

YOU WILL WIN A LARGE SUM OF MONEY.

THE RUBBER BANDS ARE HEADING IN THE RIGHT DIRECTION.

YOU ARE BETTER THAN CHOCOLATE.

PEOPLE IN YOUR LIFE WILL BE MORE HELPFUL THAN USUAL (WITH JUST A SMALL BRIBE).

MAY YOUR BOAT SOON FIND DRY LAND.

YOU ARE NOT ILLITERATE.

THE EARLY BIRD GETS THE WORM, BUT THE SECOND MOUSE GETS THE CHEESE.

SOME PURSUE HAPPINESS. YOU CREATE IT.

THE ULTIMATE TEST OF FRIENDSHIP IS TO DISAGREE BUT TO HOLD HANDS.

❧ I'D LIKE TO ❧
THANK...

Has anyone ever inspired you to do something cool, great, or difficult? Encouraged you when you wanted to give up? Cheered you on when you needed it?

WHO WOULD YOU LIKE TO THANK? LIST THE PEOPLE WHO INSPIRED YOU TO DO SOMETHING THAT YOU WERE GLAD YOU DID.

EXAMPLES TO HELP YOU OUT:

I'D LIKE TO THANK MY MOM FOR HELPING ME GET OUT OF BED EVERY MORNING!

I'D LIKE TO THANK MY GEOMETRY TEACHER FOR TEACHING ME THAT THE SQUARE OF THE LENGTH OF THE HYPOTENUSE EQUALS THE SUM OF THE SQUARES OF THE LENGTHS OF THE OTHER TWO SIDES.

I'D LIKE TO GIVE A SHOUT-OUT TO MY BEST FRIEND FOR NOT GIVING UP ON ME WHEN I FELT LIKE QUITTING.

A BIG THANKS TO MY PUPPY FOR BEING MY BEST FRIEND WHEN ALL MY HUMAN FRIENDS WERE MAD AT ME.

~ YOUR TURN ~

I'D LIKE TO THANK

_____

_____

_____

_____

_____

A BIG THANKS

_____

_____

_____

_____

_____

_____

THANK YOU

_____

_____

_____

_____

_____

A SHOUT-OUT TO

_____

_____

_____

_____

_____

THANKS

_____

_____

_____

_____

_____

_____

GRACIAS

_____

_____

_____

_____

_____

HEAD IN THE clouds

DAYDREAMING IS A SKILL! WHAT BETTER WAY TO DAYDREAM THAN TO DO A BIT OF CLOUD WATCHING?

Look at the clouds and draw what you see on the next page. Let your imagination run wild. Does your mood affect what you see? If you're in a feisty mood, perhaps you see a dragon and a warrior. If you're feeling relaxed, do you see a merry-go-round?

DRAW YOUR DAYDREAM CLOUDS.

I CAN'T Thank you ENOUGH

Have you ever had a truly amazing teacher? Wouldn't it be cool to send a secret letter to show your appreciation? Your teacher would remember it forever! Fill in the letter in the cleverest way you can think of, and stash it in your classroom for your teacher to find.

★

DEAR _____,

I wanted to take some time to _____ how much I enjoyed being in your class. I can't think of a teacher who could have made this year any more _____ than you did. You are a(n) _____ teacher because of your _____. Especially when you were teaching _____, you always made sure that we understood the _____. Without you, I never would have been able to _____. Being able to ask you for extra _____ was really _____ to me. I will never forget all the activities we did in class. I especially _____ how you always related the lessons to _____ so the new ideas made more sense to us. It made it so much easier to _____ the lessons. Thank you for a great _____ and for always going the extra mile. I appreciate it more than you will ever know.

FROM SOMEONE WHO THINKS YOU'RE _____ !

DREAM UP, DRAW,

AND DECORATE YOUR FAVORITE QUOTE

FROM A FAMOUS HISTORIC FIGURE OR LOCAL COMMUNITY MEMBER.

Think of someone whose life and work have impressed you!

Copyright © 2015
BY Nicole LaRue and Naomi Lee

ALL RIGHTS RESERVED. NO PART OF THIS BOOK
MAY BE REPRODUCED IN ANY FORM WITHOUT WRITTEN
PERMISSION FROM THE PUBLISHER.

ISBN 978-1-4521-2939-6

Manufactured in CHINA.

Text by Naomi Davis Lee.
Illustrations and design by
Nicole LaRue.

10 9 8 7 6 5 4 3

Chronicle Books LLC
680 Second Street
San Francisco, CA 94107

We see things differently. Become part of our community at
www.chroniclekids.com.